SECURITY
THE FALSE
AND THE TRUE

by

W. T. Purkiser, Ph.D.

BEACON HILL PRESS OF KANSAS CITY
Kansas City, Missouri

Copyright 1956
by Beacon Hill Press of Kansas City

Second edition 1974

ISBN 083-410-0487

Printed in the
United States of America

16   15   14   13   12   11   10   9   8

Contents

Preface

There is no question in the mind of any true child of God about the fact of his security in the Father's keeping. To say that those who do not accept one particular theory concerning Christian security are therefore without such assurance is incorrect. I do not have to be told that I cannot under any circumstances take my own life in order to be free from fear of suicide. The security of the real Christian is complete and entire, wanting nothing.

There are, however, some very false and therefore very dangerous notions abroad as to the nature of Christian security. A false security is worse than none at all, for it breeds carelessness and unfounded confidence. True security demands knowledge of the conditions on which it rests. "Wherefore let him that thinketh he standeth take heed lest he fall" (1 Cor. 10:12).

It is our firm conviction that any teaching regarding the security of the believer which allows for deliberate disobedience to God in the "Christian" life is a travesty on the Bible. Any doctrine which offers hope to the backslider that his salvation is assured apart from a personal repentance and return to the Lord is false security. Unfortunately, many who teach what is popularly known as "eternal security" teach exactly that, as numerous quotations from their writings would show. This teaching is dangerous and unscriptural. True security demands complete repudiation of such a doctrine.

No attempt is made here to cite authorities, although

care has been taken to copy word for word the passages indicated in quotation marks. It is primarily our desire to see what "saith the Lord." All Bible quotations are from the King James Version, but a check of the more recent versions will indicate that the teaching of no passage is materially altered in any good translation.

We propose to study some of the great security promises in order that their truth may safeguard our souls and keep us from presumptuous sins. "Thy word have I hid in mine heart, that I might not sin against thee" (Ps. 119:11). In this way we shall know the true security promised to all of God's children. It is not our wish to be argumentative, although argument is involved when contrasting points of view are set against each other.

Our title for this booklet is an obvious paraphrase of the title of Dr. Harry A. Ironside's book, *Holiness: the False and the True*, a book ably answered by Henry Brockett in *Scriptural Freedom from Sin* (Kansas City, Mo.: Beacon Hill Press, 1941). Brother Ironside did not believe in the Wesleyan doctrine of holiness, nor can I accept his theory of security. A more complete examination of the issues in Christian security has been made by R. A. Shank in his volume entitled *Life in the Son*. Coming as it does from evangelical circles traditionally supporting the doctrine known as eternal security, its thorough refutation of this theory is the more impressive.

—W. T. Purkiser

1

Who Are the Sheep?

My sheep hear my voice, and I know them, and they follow me: and I give unto them eternal life; and they shall never perish, neither shall any man pluck them out of my hand. My Father, which gave them me, is greater than all; and no man is able to pluck them out of my Father's hand. I and my Father are one (John 10:27-30).

This is one of God's most precious promises. Every word is sublimely true. Christ's sheep have eternal life. They shall never perish. No man can pluck them out of Christ's hand. Christ and the Father are one, and no one is able to pluck them out of the Father's hand. There is no room for foolish fears here. There is no excuse for lack of confidence on the part of any of the sheep. Whatever human failures there may be, there can never be a failure on God's part.

However, we must take God's Word as we find it, and not alter it to suit our wishes. The absolute safety of the sheep is certain. But there is another absolute statement here. In fact, Jesus puts this other statement first, so that there may be no mistake about it. He says, "My sheep hear my voice, and I know them, and they follow me."

9

This passage is a check drawn on the inexhaustible resources of the Bank of Heaven. It is made in favor of those who hear Christ's voice and follow Him. Any such believer may endorse it and cash it at face value. But let no one who is straying, or of another fold, try to cash in on this promise. The cashier is never fooled by forged signatures!

No one objects to the "perseverance of the saints." It is the "perseverance of sinners" that must be opposed. Let no man for the sake of a false security deny the plain statement of God's Word—"My sheep . . . follow me." There are no exceptions allowed. He who follows is one of the sheep. He who does not follow is not of Christ's fold no matter how loudly he may bleat his "ba-a-a's."

Further, these are all present-tense statements. "They are hearing My voice"; "They are following Me"; "I am giving eternal life"; those who are so doing "shall never perish." There is nothing in this scripture, or anywhere else in the Bible, to give false confidence to any who are not now following the Lord, whatever their past might have been. We must not wrest the Scriptures, as some do, "unto their own destruction" (2 Pet. 3:16). No one is authorized to rewrite this passage to read, "They once heard My voice and followed Me, and I give unto them eternal life." By no stretch of the imagination can these verses properly be supposed to give security to wandering, straying sheep, who go after the thief that comes to steal, kill, and destroy (v. 10).

Reduced to its simplest logic, this passage asserts:

> All who are secure are Christ's sheep;
> Those who do not follow Him are not Christ's sheep;
> Therefore, those who do not follow Him are not secure.

It should be noted that this chapter does not draw a contrast between sheep and goats. It is useless to argue that, while goats may become sheep, sheep cannot become goats. The contrast here is between Christ's sheep and those of another fold. Jesus speaks of lost sheep, the "lost sheep of the house of Israel" (Matt. 10:6; 15:24), "my sheep which was lost" (Luke 15:6). The difference is seen in the fact that Christ's sheep follow Him. Others do not.

There is true security, then, for those who follow the Lord. They are Christ's sheep. One who does not follow is not of Christ's fold. There is no comfort for such in this passage. Peter, who heard these words of the Master, spells it out for us: "For even hereunto were ye called: because Christ also suffered for us, leaving us an example, that ye should *follow* his steps: *who did no sin*, neither was guile found in his mouth . . . who his own self bare our sins in his own body on the tree, that we, *being dead to sins*, should *live unto righteousness*" (1 Pet. 2:21-24).

2

What About Separation?

Who shall separate us from the love of Christ? shall tribulation, or distress, or persecution, or famine, or nakedness, or peril, or sword? As it is written, For thy sake we are killed all the day long; we are accounted as sheep for the slaughter. Nay, in all these things we are more than conquerors through him that loved us. For I am persuaded, that neither death, nor life, nor angels, nor principalities, nor powers, nor things present, nor things to come, nor height, nor depth, nor any other creature, shall be able to separate us from the love of God, which is in Christ Jesus our Lord (Rom. 8:35-39).

This is another sublime security passage. Here again God's Word must be taken for what it says. There are no forces nor influences in heaven above, on earth, or in hell which can drive a wedge between the soul and the Saviour.

However, the Scriptures must not be made to teach false security. In Isa. 59:1-2 we are told: "Behold, the Lord's hand is not shortened, that it cannot save; neither his ear heavy, that it cannot hear: but your iniquities have separated between you and your God, and your sins have hid his face from you, that he will not hear."

Sin is not a *thing*. It is a choice, an act of a finite will. It is the suicide of the soul. It can never be a matter of compulsion. It is always avoidable. And it always brings a separation between God and man.

It is a travesty on biblical scholarship that the eighth chapter of Romans should ever be used to encourage a security that promises salvation in spite of sin. For here we read: "There is therefore now no condemnation to them which are in Christ Jesus, who walk not after the flesh, but after the Spirit. For the law of the Spirit of life in Christ Jesus hath made me free from the law of sin and death. For what the law could not do, in that it was weak through the flesh, God sending his own Son in the likeness of sinful flesh, and for sin, condemned [not, *condoned*] sin in the flesh: that the righteousness of the law might be fulfilled in us, who walk not after the flesh, but after the Spirit" (vv. 1-4).

The promises here are to those "who *walk not after the flesh*, but after the Spirit," whom "the law of the Spirit of life in Christ Jesus *hath made . . . free from the law of sin and death*," and in whom "the righteousness of the law" is fulfilled.

Sonship to God is clearly defined in verse 14, "For as many as are led by the Spirit of God, they are the sons of God." All God's sons are led by His Spirit. No one who lives in sin can claim to be led by the Spirit of God. By what stretch of the imagination, then, can such a person—whatever his past—be comforted by the statement that if he has ever been converted, though he live in sin so dreadful that

13

God must take him out of the world, he is still God's child and will be saved?

That sin separates the soul from God is the clear teaching of the Bible throughout. In 2 John 8 and 9 we are exhorted: "Look to yourselves, that we lose not those things which we have wrought, but that we receive a full reward. Whosoever transgresseth, and abideth not in the doctrine of Christ, hath not God. He that abideth in the doctrine of Christ, he hath both the Father and the Son."

Jesus himself directed His disciples to abide in Him in faithfulness, stating, "Every branch in me that beareth not fruit he taketh away. . . . If a man abide not in me, he is cast forth as a branch, and is withered; and men gather them, and cast them into the fire, and they are burned" (John 15:2, 6). It is dodging the truth to say that these are not really branches, or that God takes them away to heaven.

Paul uses the same language in Rom. 11:22: "Behold therefore the goodness and severity of God: on them which fell, severity; but toward thee, goodness, if thou continue in his goodness: *otherwise thou also shalt be cut off.*"

The writer to the Hebrews makes crystal-clear the fact that sin separates the soul from the Saviour. There are two memorable passages to be considered.

The first is Heb. 6:4-6: "For it is impossible for those who were once enlightened, and have tasted of the heavenly gift, and were made partakers of the Holy Ghost, and have tasted of the good word of God, and the powers of the world to come, *if they shall fall away*, to renew them again unto repentance; seeing they crucify to themselves the Son of God afresh, and put him to an open shame."

Some have gone to great lengths to sidestep the obvious truth of this passage. A favorite device is to deny that the persons mentioned were saved at all, even though they were enlightened and had tasted of the heavenly gift, the good word of God, and the powers of the world to come. The word "tasted" is the same word used of Jesus in Heb. 2:9 when it is said that He "tasted death for every man," and means "to have full experience of." They were also partakers of the Holy Ghost, and had a relationship with God from which to "fall away." In addition they had repented, for the expression is used, "to renew them again unto repentance." What words could better be used to describe a real if immature Christian experience?

Others argue that this is a hypothetical statement, and relates to something that could not happen. This objection, of course, completely cancels out the first argument. But the Bible nowhere gives such emphasis to something which could not possibly take place. What is the sense of warning of something which could never be?

Nor will it do to say that the passage in question cannot be reconciled with the belief in a possible recovery from backsliding. Such an objection ignores the all-important fact that the verb tense is present, and the apostle says it is impossible to renew those to repentance who *are crucifying* the Son of God afresh by their sin, and *are putting* Him to an open shame by their backsliding. In the original this is quite clear, for both verbs are present participles. Restoration is not denied to those who cease crucifying Christ afresh, and who cease putting Him to shame. The impossibility of restoration lasts as long as the crucifying and putting to shame.

The second important passage in Hebrews is the powerful warning of 10:26-29: "For if we sin [Greek, while we are sinning] wilfully after that we have received the knowledge of the truth, there remaineth no more sacrifice for sins, but a certain fearful looking for of judgment and fiery indignation, which shall devour the adversaries. He that despised Moses' law died without mercy under two or three witnesses: of how much sorer punishment, suppose ye, shall he be thought worthy, who hath trodden under foot the Son of God, and hath counted the blood of the covenant, wherewith he was sanctified, an unholy thing, and hath done despite unto the Spirit of grace?"

Here again the verb tense is present. While we are sinning willfully after having received the knowledge of the truth, there is no sacrifice for sins. The disease of sin has only one remedy. As long as we are spurning that remedy we have no hope of recovery. If you were on an island on which there was only one boat, and you refused to take that boat, you could not possibly get off the island. But every backslider has the gracious promise of Isa. 55:7: "Let the wicked forsake his way, and the unrighteous man his thoughts: and *let him return unto the Lord*, and he will have mercy upon him; and to our God, for he will abundantly pardon."

The important point to notice is that those who have received the knowledge of the truth and have been sanctified by the blood of the covenant may yet go back to willful sin, in which case they separate themselves from the redeeming grace of the Lord Jesus. To say that this refers to those who are not real Christians is to handle the Word of God deceitfully, and to condemn to eternal punishment all who fail to fully accept Christ the very first time they hear the gospel.

Peter in Acts 1:25 affirms that "Judas by transgression fell, that he might go to his own place." Some have tried to save their theory by asserting that Judas' own place was heaven, others by stating that Judas was never really saved. Again the two arguments cancel each other out. However, both are in error. Jesus stated that Judas was lost (John 17:12). His own place certainly was not heaven. If Judas were not at first a true disciple, then there is no reason to believe the others were. If he was not saved, how could he fall? That Jesus referred to him in saying, "One of you is a devil," does not prove that Judas never was a real disciple any more than the fact that Jesus said to Peter, "Get thee behind me, Satan," proves that Peter was not converted.

"Neither death, nor life, nor angels, nor principalities, nor powers, nor things present, nor things to come, nor height, nor depth, nor any other creature shall be able to separate us from the love of God, which is in Christ Jesus our Lord." Only sin and transgression can do that. And we, like Paul, can say: "The sting of death is sin; and the strength of sin is the law. But thanks be to God, which giveth us the victory through our Lord Jesus Christ" (1 Cor. 15: 55-56).

3

Sonship and Sin

Any study of the Bible doctrine of security soon runs head on into the problem of sonship to God in relation to sin. There are professed Christians who say, "I sin every day in word, thought, and deed," an achievement Satan himself cannot surpass since there are no more ways to sin than in word, thought, and deed, and it is not possible to sin any more often than every day.

Let it be quickly said that we are not talking now about faults, shortcomings, mistakes, and infirmities, which are part of our human limitation. We use the term *sin* in the only sense in which it can be used in the context of the entire New Testament, as relating to the commission or omission of something known to be the requirement of God's law, and which is within our power to avoid or to do.

If it be claimed that a true child of God will live a victorious life, and that if a professing Christian does go back into sin it is evidence he never was saved—this doctrine may not be true, but at least it is harmless. Almost invariably, however, teachers of eternal security go farther. They state that though a child of God may go back to a life of sin he is still a child of God and is assured of final salvation by that fact, even while he is living in open rebellion against God. •

Much of this teaching rests upon a mistaken application of the father-son relationship. We are definitely told in 1 Cor. 2:13 to beware of the danger of false analogies and instead to compare "spiritual things with spiritual."

"Once a son, always a son," it is argued. But this metaphor proves too much. It proves that we can never be saved in the first place, for we are all born "children of wrath" (Eph. 2:3), and "children of the devil" (1 John 3:10). If once born into a family we could never cease to be children of that family, then we must always be children of disobedience.

Again we hear, "Once born, one can never be unborn." True enough. But the logical contradictory of birth is not unbirth, but death. A child may die. "Adam . . . was the son of God" (Luke 3:38); yet God said, "In the day that thou eatest thereof thou shalt surely die" (Gen. 2:17). False security was offered, even in the Garden, for the serpent assured the woman, "Ye shall not surely die" (Gen. 3:4).

It is argued that the prodigal wasting his substance with harlots and in riotous living was still a son. But Jesus said he was dead, and lost (Luke 15:24, 32). Wherein is a dead son and a lost son any better off than no son at all? James says, "Brethren, if any of *you* do err from the truth, and one convert him; let him know, that he which converteth the sinner from the error of his way shall save a soul from death, and shall hide a multitude of sins" (5:19-20).

This matter is so important it deserves careful study. Let us see what the Bible has to say concerning the claim that one who goes back into sin or who continues in sin may yet be assured of final salvation as a child of God. Such teaching, in the words of Ezek. 13:22, strengthens "the hands of the wicked, that he should not *return* from his wicked way, *by promising him life.*"

We are speaking now, of course, of the person commonly known as the "backslider." There are many who may be classed as backsliders who have never "climbed forward," whose religion was only a matter of human reformation. These, of course, do not concern us here. We speak of those who themselves are convinced that they really knew the Lord, but who have turned away from His known will for their lives. It is claimed, "God punishes His children when they sin, but they are His children still,"[1] and,

> once a poor sinner has been regenerated by the Word and the Spirit of God, once he has received a new life and a new nature, has been made partaker of the divine nature, once he has been justified from every charge before the throne of God, it is absolutely impossible that that man should ever again be a lost soul.[2]

The question is, Can a child of God live in sin? Or conversely, Can one who lives in sin (as a backslider, by definition, does) be a child of God, and thus a saved person? For this we seek an answer in the Word.

Our very first New Testament introduction to Christ is in the words of the angelic prediction, "And thou shalt call his name JESUS: for he shall save his people *from* their sins" (Matt. 1:21). One would look long and far to find any scriptural warrant for the notion that Christ saves anyone *in* his sins. If a person isn't saved *from* his sins, he isn't saved.

Jesus tells us that the moral quality of the life is the only true indication of the spiritual state of the heart. "A good tree cannot bring forth evil fruit, neither can a corrupt tree bring forth good fruit. Every tree that bringeth not forth good fruit is hewn down, and cast into the fire. Wherefore by their fruits ye shall know them" (Matt. 7:18-20). "Either make the tree good, and his fruit good; or else make the tree corrupt, and his fruit corrupt: for the tree is known by his fruit" (Matt. 12:33).

20

In John 8:34-36, Jesus said, "Verily, verily, I say unto you, Whosoever committeth sin is the servant of sin. . . . If the Son therefore shall make you free, ye shall be free indeed." The contrast is complete: slavery to sin or freedom in Christ. No child of God is the slave of sin. No child of God can live in sin.

Paul views as all but incredible the idea that one who knows the grace of God can live in sin: "What shall we say then? Shall we continue in sin, that grace may abound? God forbid. How shall we, that are dead to sin, live any longer therein?" (Rom. 6:1-2). "For sin shall not have dominion over you: for ye are not under the law, but under grace. What then? shall we sin, because we are not under the law, but under grace? God forbid. Know ye not, that to whom ye yield yourselves servants to obey, his servants ye are to whom ye obey; whether of sin unto death, or of obedience unto righteousness?" (Rom. 6:14-16).

But did not Paul speak of those saved "so as by fire"? He did state that those who build a structure of perishable materials on the foundation of Jesus Christ will lose the reward of an enduring lifework, but they themselves will be saved. He did not imply, however, that this could be a life of sin, for in the very next two verses he continues: "Know ye not that ye are the temple of God, and that the Spirit of God dwelleth in you? If any man defile the temple of God, him shall God destroy; for the temple of God is holy, which temple ye are" (1 Cor. 3:16-17).

In Gal. 5:19-21, Paul gives us a list of the works of the flesh. Included are many grosser sins, but also some of the more "polite" sort: hatred, wrath, strife, envyings, revelings, and suchlike. He then adds, "Of the which I tell you before, as I have also told you in time past, that *they which do such things* shall not inherit the kingdom of God."

A similar warning is found in Eph. 5:5-7: "For this ye know, that no whoremonger, nor unclean person, nor covetous man, who is an idolater, hath any inheritance in the kingdom of Christ and of God. Let no man deceive you with vain words: for because of these things cometh the wrath of God upon the children of disobedience. Be not ye therefore partakers with them." There is no exception here for those who were once believers. There is only the unqualified assurance that those who practice such sins have no inheritance in Christ's kingdom.

In 2 Peter 2 we find a description of the reprobate soul who "cannot cease from sin" (v. 14), while the terrible effects of false teaching in the Church are described in strong words in verses 18-22: "For when they speak great swelling words of vanity, they allure through the lusts of the flesh, through much wantonness, those that were clean escaped from them who live in error. While they promise them liberty, they themselves are the servants of corruption: for of whom a man is overcome, of the same is he brought in bondage. For if after they have escaped the pollutions of the world through the knowledge of the Lord and Saviour Jesus Christ, they are again entangled therein, and overcome, the latter end is worse with them than the beginning. For it had been better for them not to have known the way of righteousness, than, after they have known it, to turn from the holy commandment delivered unto them. But it is happened unto them according to the true proverb, The dog is turned to his own vomit again; and the sow that was washed to her wallowing in the mire."

Those who are again entangled with the pollutions of the world and who turn from the holy commandment find a latter end worse than the beginning. It would have been better for them never to have made the start.

It is in John's First Epistle that we find some of the strongest statements concerning the incompatibility of a life of sin with the Christian hope. Although other New Testament writers leave no doubt, John was confronted with a heresy which resembles the false security of our day in some rather startling ways. It was being taught that the body is the seat and source of sin, and that the soul might be redeemed and pure while the physical nature is corrupt and sinful. John, on the other hand, regarded the Gnostic sophistry as false profession and a fabric of lies. What he says about it applies with equal force to any teaching which would state or imply that it is possible for a soul to be saved from future wrath by a past experience of the new birth while that person is living in sin or transgressing God's law.

"If we say that we have fellowship with him, and walk in darkness, we lie, and do not the truth: but if we walk in the light, as he is in the light, we have fellowship one with another, and the blood of Jesus Christ his Son cleanseth us from all sin" (1 John 1:6-7). The next verse does not contradict what has just been said, but rather states, "If we say that we have no sin [from which to be cleansed, as in verse 7], we deceive ourselves."

The whole purpose of John's writing is to counteract the notion of the possibility and necessity of "sinning sainthood." "My little children, these things write I unto you, that ye sin not" (2:1). Even the provision made for the soul entrapped into a momentary sin, immediately renounced and not repeated, carries the clear statement that sin is not necessary: "And IF [not, when] any man sin, we have an advocate with the Father, Jesus Christ the righteous: and he is the propitiation for our sins: and not for ours only, but also for the sins of the whole world" (2:1-2).

The original Greek here clearly shows that John is not talking about repeated sinning "every day in word, thought, and deed." He rather gives encouragement to the soul impulsively plunged into some sin under the pressure of strong temptation, who immediately confesses and renounces his sin and avails himself of the services of the Advocate for his forgiveness. Such sin as this, thus renounced, causes only a momentary break with the Father. If repeated and rationalized, far more tragic results follow.

John gives little comfort to those who profess to know God, but who live in unrighteousness. "He that saith, I know him, and keepeth not his commandments, is a liar, and the truth is not in him" (2:4). A religious experience which does not save from sin, according to John, is a sham and a fraud. "And ye know that he was manifested to take away our sins; and in him is no sin. Whosoever abideth in him sinneth not: whosoever sinneth hath not seen him, neither known him" (3:5-6).

John also gives a direct and unqualified answer to the question, Can one who lives in sin (as a backslider) be a child of God? "He that committeth sin is of the devil; for the devil sinneth from the beginning. For this purpose the Son of God was manifested, that he might destroy the works of the devil. Whosoever is born of God doth not commit sin; for his seed remaineth in him: and he cannot sin, because he is born of God" (3:8-9). "We know that whosoever is born of God sinneth not; but he that is begotten of God keepeth himself, and that wicked one toucheth him not" (5:18).

Some have been puzzled, to be sure, by the words in 3:9, "He cannot sin, because he is born of God." This does not say that the child of God is *not able to* sin. What it says is that he is *able not to* sin.

The seed of God and the principle of sin are logically contradictory moral qualities, just as truthfulness and lying, honesty and theft, patriotism and treason—and cannot exist together. A truthful man *cannot* lie, not because he has no lips and tongue and mind to frame falsehood, but because if he lies he is not a truthful man. An honest man *cannot* steal, not because he has no desires and hands and opportunities to take what does not belong to him, but because if he steals he is not an honest man. A patriot *cannot* commit treason, not because he is physically incapable thereof, but because if he engages in treasonable acts he is not a patriot. Nowhere in all God's universe is there such a creature as a truthful liar, an honest thief, or a loyal traitor. Nor, in John's trenchant terms, is there anywhere in God's universe a sinning saint. "He that committeth sin is of the devil."

It thus becomes evident that sin and sonship to God are contradictory terms. To affirm otherwise is to fly right in the face of God's Word.

Here the doctrine of eternal security faces an impossible dilemma. It must either affirm that backsliding is impossible, that one born of God cannot possibly fall back into sin or live in conscious rebellion against God. Or it must deny the clear and oft repeated statement of God's Word that the child of God does not commit sin. The former alternative virtually nullifies the practical meaning of the doctrine, for it just says to the new convert, "If you follow Christ, you are really saved; if you do not, you did not have anything in the first place." Unfortunately, it is the second option that is usually taken—the idea that sin and sonship are compatible.

True security, on the other hand, recognizes the adequacy of divine grace, redeeming, sanctifying, and keeping from sin. "For the grace of God that bringeth salvation hath appeared to all men, teaching us that, denying ungodliness and worldly lusts, we should live soberly, righteously, and godly, in this present world; looking for that blessed hope, and the glorious appearing of the great God and our Saviour Jesus Christ; who gave himself for us, that he might redeem us from all iniquity, and purify unto himself a peculiar people, zealous of good works" (Titus 2:11-14).

True security possesses the added merit of recognizing the fact that the adversary does not give up when one is converted. It does not, ostrich-like, bury its head in the sand and deny the existence of any real peril to the soul. Its strength is greater because its realism keeps it alert and constantly dependent on God for daily help and sustaining grace. "Keep

25

yourselves in the love of God. . . . Now unto him that is able to keep you" (Jude 21, 24) expresses the twofold security of the trusting child of God.

4

Believed or Believing?

The Bible is a Book of incredibly accurate detail. This is seen particularly in the care with which verb tenses are written. Scripture writers never put an action in the present tense unless it represents something now going on. This is especially true of the many references to saving faith found in the New Testament. Almost without exception they are in the present tense—referring to something begun at a given time and *now going on.*

Many examples may be given. A few from John's Gospel will suffice.

John 3:16, "That whosoever believeth [present tense, is believing] in him should not perish, but have everlasting life."

John 5:24, "Verily, verily, I say unto you, He that heareth [present tense, is hearing] my word, and believeth [is believing] on him that sent me, hath everlasting life, and shall not come into condemnation; but is passed from death unto life."

John 6:35, "He that believeth [present tense, is believing] on me shall never thirst."

John 11:26, "Whosoever liveth [is living] and believeth [is believing] in me shall never die."

John 20:30, "But these are written that ye might believe that Jesus is the Christ, the Son of God; and that believing ye might have life through his name."

The doctrine of eternal security makes the mistake of ignoring God's present tenses and changes them to the past tense. Quoting John 5:24, one wrote, "If you have trusted in Christ, you now have eternal life, everlasting life, life that will last forever, and you will not lose it!"[1] Substituting man's past tense for God's present tense looks like a small thing, but how radically it alters the truth of the Bible! Jesus *did not say*, "If you *have trusted*." He said, "If you *are trusting*." These are poles apart in meaning. To suppose that this careful use of the present tense instead of the past is accidental is to charge God's inspired penman with writing what he did not mean.

We must now examine this assumption that one single act of faith, whatever follows, forever secures eternal life, or as one has put it, secures a paid-up, nonforfeitable life insurance policy. True security rests on the scriptural conviction that it is present-tense, up-to-date faith which pleases God (Heb. 11:6) and secures eternal life (1 John 5:10-12).

Properly speaking, a believer is one who now believes, not one who may at some time in the past have believed. Believing is a process, a continued action. One may have believed in Santa Claus as a child, but that fact does not make him a believer in St. Nick at the present time. Faith represents an attitude and activity of the soul which may change in the course of a person's life.

Nowhere does the Bible suggest that a person who one time believed in Christ is by that past-tense faith assured of final salvation. Eph. 1:13 is often wrongly quoted in this connection, "In whom ye also trusted, after that ye heard the word of truth, the gospel of your salvation: in whom also af-

28

ter that ye believed, ye were sealed with that holy Spirit of promise." This does not suggest that the Ephesians had ceased or could cease trusting and believing and still retain God's seal. In fact, in Eph. 4:30, Paul distinctly rejects such a notion, indicating that the seal is the continued presence of the Holy Spirit: "And grieve not the holy Spirit of God, *whereby ye are* sealed unto the day of redemption."

The New Testament contains many passages which warn against forsaking that present-tense faith which alone secures salvation. Jesus in Luke 8:13 describes the quick-sprouting seed on the rock as representing those who "when they hear, receive the word with joy; and these have no root, which *for a while believe*, and in time of temptation fall away."

In John 8:31, "Then said Jesus to those Jews which believed on him, If ye continue in my word, then are ye my disciples indeed." Even though they *had* believed, they must continue if they were to be His disciples indeed.

Again in John 3:18 we read, "He that believeth [is believing] on him is not condemned: but he that believeth not [is not believing] is condemned already, because he hath not believed [Greek, he is not in the abiding condition or state of being of believing] in the name of the only begotten Son of God."

In one of His great parables, recorded in Luke 12:42-47, Jesus speaks of the judgment which awaits His coming. He states that the servant is blessed who is found faithfully discharging his duties at his lord's return, and shall be made ruler over all the master has. "But and if," says Jesus, "*that servant* say in his heart, My lord delayeth his coming; and shall begin to beat the menservants and maidens, and to eat and drink, and to be drunken; the lord of that servant will come in a day when he looketh not for him, and at an hour when he is not aware, and will cut him in sunder, and will appoint him his portion with the unbelievers."

It will not do to brush this off with the comment that it speaks of "servants and not sons." Jesus makes it perfectly clear that the only difference between the servant who was blessed and the servant who was condemned was in faithfulness, and the condemned servant has his portion "with the unbelievers."

That more than initial faith is necessary is seen in the story of Simon, who in Acts 8:13 is said to have believed and been baptized, but whose later lust for power and position in the church led Peter to call upon him to repent, lest he and his money both perish (vv. 21-22).

Paul stresses the imperative need of continued faith in Rom. 11:20-22: "Well, because of unbelief they were broken off, and thou standest by faith. Be not highminded, but fear: for if God speared not the natural branches, take heed lest he also spare not thee. Behold therefore the goodness and severity of God: on them which fell, severity; but toward thee, goodness, if thou continue in his goodness: otherwise thou also shalt be cut off." To say that this is addressed to the Gentile church and not to individuals is utterly to miss the point. For the church is nothing apart from the persons who compose it, and cannot lose the faith and be cut off except as its individual members lose the faith and are cut off.

To the Corinthians, Paul writes: "Moreover, brethren, I declare unto you the gospel which I preached unto you, which also ye have received, and wherein ye stand; by which also ye are saved, if ye keep in memory what I preached unto you, unless ye have believed in vain" (1 Cor. 15:1-2). Here the standing of the disciples is plainly stated to be in continued faith. Failing this, their initial faith would be in vain, which could never be said if that first faith guaranteed final salvation. "By faith ye stand" (2 Cor. 1:24).

Paul speaks of the purpose of God to "present you holy and unblameable and unreproveable in his sight: *if ye con-*

tinue in the faith grounded and settled, and be not moved away from the hope of the gospel, which ye have heard, and which was preached to every creature which is under heaven; whereof I Paul am made a minister" (Col. 1:22-23).

Also concerned about the perseverance of the Thessalonians, Paul tells them, "For this cause, when I could no longer forbear, I sent to know your faith, lest by some means the tempter have tempted you, and our labour be in vain" (1 Thess. 3:5). Since no labor which resulted in the final salvation of these Christians could be in vain, Paul evidently did not believe that their first single act of saving faith was all that was necessary to get them to heaven.

In his first letter to Timothy, Paul reveals his concern over those who have believed, and were being tempted to leave the faith. He does not assume that "having once trusted in Christ" they could not possibly be lost. "This charge I commit unto thee, son Timothy, according to the prophecies which went before on thee, that thou by them mightest war a good warfare; holding faith, and a good conscience; which some having put away concerning faith have made shipwreck: of whom is Hymenaeus and Alexander; whom I have delivered unto Satan, that they may learn not to blaspheme" (1 Tim. 1:18-20). "Now the Spirit speaketh expressly, that in the latter times some shall depart from the faith, giving heed to seducing spirits, and doctrines of devils" (4:1). The social evils to which young widows were exposed led to this warning: "But the younger widows refuse: for when they have begun to wax wanton against Christ, they will marry; having damnation, because they have cast off their first faith. . . . For some have already turned aside after Satan" (5:11-12, 15).

Timothy himself is told to "fight the good fight of faith, lay hold on eternal life, whereunto thou art also called, and hast professed a good profession before many witnesses" (1 Tim. 6:12). Eternal life, apparently, is not a cut-and-dried

31

affair sealed at conversion, unless it be alleged that Timothy was not yet born again.

The writer to the Hebrews likewise emphasizes the need for continuing faith to assure final salvation. "Take heed, brethren, lest there be in any of you an evil heart of unbelief, in departing from the living God. But exhort one another daily, while it is called To day; lest any of you be hardened through the deceitfulness of sin. For we are made partakers of Christ, if we hold fast the beginning of our confidence stedfast unto the end" (3:12-14; see also v. 6). These are the persons addressed in verse 1 as "holy brethren." Departing from the living God reveals an evil heart of unbelief. To say that this means only to "show that you were truly saved by continuing in the faith" actually surrenders the case for eternal security. For if those who depart thus were never truly saved, what guarantee has anyone now in the faith that some future lapse of his may not show him to have been deluded all the time?

Again in Heb. 10:38-39 we read: "Now the just shall live by faith: but if any man draw back, my soul shall have no pleasure in him. But we are not of them who draw back unto perdition; but of them that believe to the saving of the soul." Here also living by faith and continuing to believe are made the basis for final salvation.

A final point is found in the fact that the real evidence of a true and living faith is the quality of the life. Whoever claims to have a saving faith in Christ and at the same time lives in sin is making a patently false profession. For it is not what we say about it but what we do that demonstrates the reality of our faith. The moral quality of the life is the final test of whether or not we are believing or bluffing. "Faith, if it have not works, is dead, being alone. . . . But wilt thou know, O vain man, that faith without works is dead?" (Jas. 2:17, 20).

True security rests in the fact that saving faith is not a

single historical act, but a present-tense, up-to-date, continuing process. Every believer has eternal life, and that life is correlated with the faith by which he lives. "I am crucified with Christ: nevertheless I live; yet not I, but Christ liveth in me: and the life which I now live in the flesh I live by the faith of the Son of God, who loved me, and gave himself for me" (Gal. 2:20). It is the shield of faith which quenches every fiery dart of the enemy and assures of true security (Eph. 6:16).

5

Salvation—Free, Full and Final

Confusion always comes when we forget that temporal salvation and final salvation are not one and the same thing. The claim that everyone saved temporally will by that fact be saved finally is without biblical support. In fact, the Word clearly teaches that some who were "saved" temporally may not be saved eternally.

That final salvation is not guaranteed by an initial experience of saving faith is clearly shown in Rom. 13:11, where we read, "And that, knowing the time, that now it is high time to awake out of sleep: *for now is our salvation nearer than when we believed.*" Believing brings temporal salvation. Continuing to believe insures final salvation.

In 1 Pet. 1:5, 9, and 13, the writer speaks of a final salvation which is not the present possession of believers here and now: "Who are kept by the power of God through faith unto salvation ready to be revealed in the last time." "Receiving the end of your faith, even the salvation of your souls." "Wherefore gird up the loins of your mind, be sober, and hope to the end for the grace that is to be brought unto you at the revelation of Jesus Christ."

Three times we find a record of Jesus' statement, "He that shall endure unto the end, the same shall be saved" (Matt. 10:22; 24:13; and Mark 13:13). Jesus spoke of the days in which we live, when iniquity abounds, and the love of many in the Church gradually becomes cold (Matt. 24:12).

Paul speaks of his unremitting labors to insure the continuance of his numerous charges: "Therefore I endure all things for the elect's sakes, that they may also obtain the salvation which is in Christ Jesus with eternal glory. It is a faithful saying: For if we be dead with him, we shall also live with him: if we suffer, we shall also reign with him: if we deny him, he also will deny us" (2 Tim. 2:10-12). He then adds in verse 13, "If we believe not, yet he abideth faithful: he cannot deny himself." That is, whether or not we believe it, His Word stands true, and what He says will certainly come to pass.

Who are the elect of whom Paul speaks? The scriptural doctrine of election is that God has, of His own gracious purpose, elected to eternal life all who savingly and persistently believe on the Lord Jesus Christ. Thus Peter, after listing the graces which must be added to faith, says, "Wherefore the rather, brethren, give diligence to make your calling and election sure: for if ye do these things, ye shall never fall" (2 Pet. 1:10).

Salvation as the free gift of God's grace is our Christian heritage now: "For by grace are ye saved through faith; and that not of yourselves: it is the gift of God" (Eph. 2:8). This salvation may be made complete and full here in this life. "Wherefore he is able also to save them to the uttermost that come unto God by him, seeing he ever liveth to make intercession for them" (Heb. 7:25). "But we are bound to give thanks alway to God for you, brethren beloved of the Lord, because God hath from the beginning chosen you to salvation through sanctification of the Spirit and belief of the truth" (2 Thess. 2:13).

Final salvation, "the end of your faith" (1 Pet. 1:9), is "when the chief Shepherd shall appear, [and] ye shall receive a crown of glory that fadeth not away" (1 Pet. 5:4). The promises of final salvation are to the overcomer: "He that overcometh, the same shall be clothed in white raiment; and I will not blot his name out of the book of life, but I will confess his name before my Father, and before his angels" (Rev. 3:5).

If anyone might have presumed that his present salvation inevitably guaranteed his final salvation, it would have been the Apostle Paul. On the contrary, he states in 1 Cor. 9:27, "But I keep under my body, and bring it into subjection:lest that by any means, when I have preached to others, I myself should be a castaway."

One cannot say, "Paul meant 'disallowed,' and was talking about his works only." He uses the very same word here translated "castaway" in Rom. 1:28, where it is translated "reprobate"; in 2 Cor. 13:5, "Jesus Christ is in you, except ye be reprobates"; in 2 Tim. 3:8, where he speaks of false prophets as "men of corrupt minds, reprobate concerning the faith"; and in Titus 1:16, "They profess that they know God; but in works they deny him, being abominable, and disobedient, and unto every good work reprobate." In each case the word denotes those who are lost.

Paul was very jealous for the influence Christians have over the lives and destinies of their fellow Christians. Twice he alluded to this in the strongest possible terms. In Rom. 14:15, he says, "But if thy brother be grieved with thy meat, now walkest thou not charitably. Destroy not him with thy meat, for whom Christ died." Again in 1 Cor. 8:10-11: "For if any man see thee which hast knowledge sit at meat in the idol's temple, shall not the conscience of him which is weak be emboldened to eat those things which are offered to idols; and through thy knowledge shall the weak brother perish, for whom Christ died?" In both of these passages, Paul indicates that a brother for whom Christ died may be led into compromising his own convictions and eventually perish.

Peter in similar vein speaks of those who wrest the Scriptures unto their own destruction, and immediately adds, "Ye therefore, beloved, seeing ye know these things before, beware lest ye also, being led away with the error of the wicked, fall from your own stedfastness" (2 Pet. 3:17).

It is often argued that, if a child of God could be lost, the faithfulness of God would fail, and His redemptive purpose would be thwarted. As a matter of fact, the faithfulness of God would fail if any person who died in sin should be saved. God's sovereign purpose is to save every son of Adam's race who will believe and obey Him. It is also His sovereign purpose to take "vengeance on them that know not God [cf. 1 John 2:4], and that obey not the gospel of our Lord Jesus Christ: who shall be punished with everlasting destruction from the presence of the Lord, and from the glory of his power" (2 Thess. 1:8-9).

Actually, the doctrine of eternal security when based upon the sovereignty of God leads either to belief in a limited atonement or to belief in the universal salvation of all men. But God is no less faithful by reason of the fact that of His own sovereign grace He has purposed to save eternally all those who persistently believe on the Lord Jesus Christ, the genuineness of whose faith is demonstrated by their lives.

If temporal salvation and final salvation are not identical, wherein then lies our assurance of eternal life? We have it in the words of no less than Jesus himself, "Be thou faithful unto death, and I will give thee a crown of life" (Rev. 2:10); "Behold, I come quickly: hold that fast which thou hast, that no man take thy crown" (Rev. 3:11); "To him that overcometh will I grant to sit with me in my throne, even as I also overcame, and am set down with my Father in his throne" (Rev. 3:21).

True security stresses the importance of full salvation as a means of assuring final salvation. Full salvation means full deliverance from the "law of sin and death" through the "law of the Spirit of life in Christ Jesus" (Rom. 8:2). It means having the "old man" crucified with Christ, "that the body of sin might be destroyed, that henceforth we should not serve sin" (Rom 6:6). It means being "filled with the Spirit" (Eph. 5:18). And it means following "peace with all men, and holiness, without which no man shall see the Lord: looking diligently lest any man fail of [marg., fall back from] the grace of God; lest any root of bitterness springing up trouble you, and thereby many be defiled" (Heb. 12:14-15). In this path is true security for every child of God.

6

The Meaning
of Eternal Life

Many gracious promises of eternal life are found in the Bible. Some of these have primary reference to the future state, but others speak of eternal life as now given to the believer. A number of these from the Gospel of John have been quoted in an earlier section.

These promises have been made one of the bases of a mistaken doctrine. It is asserted that eternal life has no end; therefore if one has God's gift of eternal life he can never be lost; otherwise the life would not be eternal. It might be asked in passing whether a pearl of great price might not still be a genuine pearl, and even without end, though it be lost by a careless and self-confident owner.

But the real issue lies in the right understanding of the nature of eternal life and the teaching of the Bible concerning it. Again the crucial question is whether anyone who lives a life of sin may claim to be in possession of eternal life because he once believed. Jesus said, "Father, the hour is come; glorify thy Son, that thy Son also may glorify thee: as thou hast given him power over all flesh, that he should give eternal life to as many as thou hast given him. And this is life eternal, that they might know thee the only true God, and Jesus Christ, whom thou hast sent" (John 17:1-3). And John states, "He that saith, I know him, and keepeth not his commandments, is a liar, and the truth is not in him" (1 John 2: 4).

Thus, eternal life is not merely unending existence. It has primary reference to the *quality* of life, and not to its *duration*. According to the orthodox view, the finally impenitent will exist forever in a conscious state. But their existence is called "the second death" because they are forever separated from God, the Source of spiritual life. Eternal life is in Christ, as John says: "And this is the record, that God hath given to us eternal life, and this life is in his Son. He that hath the Son hath life; and he that hath not the Son of God hath not life." "Whosoever transgresseth, and abideth not in the doctrine of Christ, hath not God. He that abideth in the doctrine of Christ, he hath both the Father and the Son" (1 John 5:11-12; 2 John 9).

Eternal life, therefore, is not something abstract and separable from the abiding presence of Christ. Christ "only hath immortality" (1 Tim. 6:16) as inherent in His nature. Our immortality is conditioned by and derived from Him. "He that hath not the Son of God hath not life," whatever his past state might have been.

It is obvious, of course, that a living being may die. In Rom. 8:13, Paul states, "If ye live after the flesh, ye shall die: but if ye through the Spirit do mortify the deeds of the body, ye shall live." This plainly is not physical death, for "it is appointed unto man once to die" (Heb. 9:27), faithful Christian men as well as all others. This is spiritual death, whose genealogy is clearly given in Jas. 1:14-16: "But every man [including the Christian man] is tempted, when he is drawn away of his own lust, and enticed. Then when lust hath conceived, it bringeth forth sin: and sin, when it is finished, bringeth forth death. Do not err, *my beloved brethren.*"

To whom then does God give eternal life?

Jesus answers, "Verily, verily, I say unto you, If a man keep my saying, he shall never see death" (John 8:51).

Paul replies that God "will render to every man according to his deeds: to them who by patient continuance in well doing seek for glory and honour and immortality, eternal life" (Rom. 2:6-7).

The writer to the Hebrews states that Christ is "the author of eternal salvation unto all them that obey him" (5:9).

"Let that therefore abide in you, which ye have heard from the beginning. If that which ye have heard from the beginning shall remain in you, ye also shall continue in the Son, and in the Father. And this is the promise that he hath promised us, even eternal life" (1 John 2:24-25).

This is an impressive array of clear-cut, unambiguous answers. Who has and shall have eternal life? Those who keep Christ's sayings; those who by patient continuance in well doing seek for glory and honor and immortality; those who obey the Lord; and those who continue in the Son and in the Father.

We have already noted that Timothy was exhorted to "lay hold on eternal life" (1 Tim. 6:12), a statement quite without meaning if every believer has the inalienable gift of final salvation. More than that, John clearly states that anyone who hates "his brother is a murderer: and ye know that no murderer hath eternal life abiding in him" (1 John 3:15).

One of the most solemn passages in the Book is 1 John 5:16: "If any man see his brother sin a sin which is not unto death, he shall ask, and he shall give him life for them that sin not unto death. There is a sin unto death: I do not say that he shall pray for it."

Only by taking this completely out of context can it be said, as some teachers of false security affirm, that John here

41

speaks only of physical death as a result of "sin in a believer's life so serious that God cannot permit such an one to continue to live on earth." One noted advocate of this teaching says: "This may mean for such to be taken away by death, because they so dishonor the name of Christ that they can no longer be permitted to remain on earth. They are redeemed by the blood of Christ and thus fit to go to heaven, but their lives are so displeasing to God that they cannot be allowed to remain on earth."[1]

It is difficult to have confidence in the thinking of anyone who would so wrest the Scriptures and pervert the Word of God. John's whole concern in this passage is eternal life (vv. 11, 13, 20), the life of the soul (v. 12), a life lost only and always by sin (v. 16).

Every follower of the Lord Jesus rejoices in the hope described in 1 John 3:1-3: "Behold, what manner of love the Father hath bestowed upon us, that we should be called the sons of God: therefore the world knoweth us not, because it knew him not. Beloved, now are we the sons of God, and it doth not yet appear what we shall be: but we know that, when he shall appear, we shall be like him; for we shall see him as he is. And every man that hath this hope in him purifieth himself, even as he is pure."

Let no one ignore the plain statement of verse 3, that all who have this hope purify themselves as Christ is pure. He who does not purify himself does not have this hope in him.

The application is obvious to the claim that Christians may "so dishonor the name of Christ that they can no longer be permitted to remain on earth," though they are "redeemed by the blood of Christ and thus fit to go to heaven." There is danger, in such teaching as this, of falling into "strong delusion, that they should believe a lie: that they all might be damned who believed not the truth, but had pleasure in unrighteousness" (2 Thess. 2:11-12).

True security for the trusting soul is found in the "path

of the just," which "shineth more and more unto the perfect day" (Prov. 4:18). While no sinning "saint" has the right to hope for eternal life, no obedient believer need fear the tempter's power. "There hath no temptation taken you but such as is common to man: but God is faithful, who will not suffer you to be tempted above that ye are able: but will with the temptation also make a way to escape, that ye may be able to bear it" (1 Cor. 10:13).

7

What About Eternal Justification?

It is sometimes claimed that "when I came to the Lord Jesus Christ and put my trust in Him, not only were all my sins up to the day of my conversion forgiven, but all my sins were put away for eternity."[1] That is, God not only justifies the soul in relation to past sins; at the same moment He also forgives all future sins that will ever be committed.

This, it is said, is because the sacrifice of Christ was an eternal sacrifice, and it is by the sacrifice of Christ that we are justified. The scripture is quoted, "For by one offering he hath perfected for ever them that are sanctified" (Heb. 10:14). Characteristically, the stress is laid on the words "for ever," and the fact is ignored that this concerns those who *are* sanctified, not those who have been sanctified in some past time. One should also note that it is the same chapter which cautions us against willful sin after receiving the knowledge of the truth (v. 26), and which brings the solemn warning already quoted, "Of how much sorer pun-

44

ishment, suppose ye, shall he be thought worthy, who hath trodden under foot the Son of God, and hath counted the blood of the covenant, wherewith he *was sanctified*, an unholy thing, and hath done despite unto the Spirit of grace?" (v. 29).

Again, it is argued that because all of our sins were in the future at the time Christ died, and since His death is the ground of our justification, therefore the one act of our justification clears us of the guilt of all our sins, past, present, and future.

This is a confusion between the atonement as the ground of justification and redemption as the actual appropriation of justification. The fact that all of our sins were in the future at the time of Christ's atonement is totally immaterial. Our sins were not forgiven *at the time* of Christ's death. We were not justified when He said, "It is finished." What was finished was the supreme and eternal and perfect work of Christ in providing the basis for our justification, "that he might be just, and the justifier of him which believeth in Jesus" (Rom. 3:26). Christ on the Cross offered to God a perfect substitute for the penalty which should have been inflicted upon us. We become partakers of His sufficient grace when and only when we savingly believe in the Lord Jesus Christ.

Justification is judicial forgiveness and takes place the moment we accept God's gracious gift of salvation in Jesus Christ, not at the time Christ died on the Cross. Our sins were not remitted at Calvary. They were remitted at conversion. The idea of justification in respect to sins which have not yet been committed is without any intelligible meaning, and directly contrary to the teachings of God's Word. In his great justification passage in Romans 3, Paul clearly and distinctly states that justification is "for the remission of *sins that are past*" (v. 25)

It is said in this connection that the Christian is not given license to sin, because God as his Father will punish his sins here in this life, although God as his Judge has already granted him forgiveness. We are told: "The moment you trust the Lord Jesus as your Saviour, your responsibility as a sinner having to do with the God of judgment is ended for eternity, but that same moment your responsibility as a child having to do with a Father in heaven begins. Now if as a child you should sin against your Father, God will have to deal with you about that, but as a Father and not as a Judge."[2]

But God is not a split personality, condoning sin as a Judge and punishing it as a Father. How could God as a Father punish what God as a Judge has already forgiven? The sinning "saint" must confess his sins in order to restore fellowship with the Father, we are told. How can the saint confess what in point of fact is already forgiven, from which he has been justified, and which by that token is as though it had never been? If they are already forgiven, there can be no punishment of a believer's sins, even by his Father—nothing more than sin's natural consequences would follow.

Again, is there any reason to suppose that God as our Heavenly Father is either more or less just than God as a Judge? If God as a Father *must deal with* the sins of His "children," how can He justly deal with them in any sense differently from that in which He deals with the sins of other men as the Judge of all the earth (Gen. 18:25)?

God does deal with our future at conversion. He does not deal with it by a blanket forgiveness of all future sins before they are committed, but by regenerating and sanctifying grace to enable us to live above sin. The careful student of the Word will note that God always conjoins justification and righteousness, never justification and future sinning. Thus, Paul says in Rom. 5:18-19: "Therefore as by one man's disobedience many were made sinners, so by the righteousness of one the free gift came upon all men unto justification of life. For as by one man's disobedience many were

46

made sinners, so by the obedience of one shall many be made righteous."

That this righteousness is not of some imaginary, "imputed" sort which leaves the soul fettered by sin is seen in 1 John 3:7, "Little children, let no man deceive you: he that doeth righteousness is righteous, *even as he is righteous*"; and in 1 Pet. 1:15, "But as he which hath called you is holy, so be ye holy in all manner of conversation [Greek, 'all manner of life']."

But we are not left without direct scriptural evidence on this point. Although the entire teaching of the Old Testament is nullified by "dispensational" arguments, those who believe that all scripture is profitable will ponder carefully Ezek. 33:12-13, 18: "Therefore, thou son of man, say unto the children of thy people, The righteousness of the righteous shall not deliver him in the day of his transgression: as for the wickedness of the wicked, he shall not fall thereby in the day that he turneth from his wickedness; neither shall the righteous be able to live for his righteousness in the day that he sinneth. When I shall say to the righteous, that he shall surely live; if he trust to his own righteousness, and commit iniquity, all his righteousness shall not be remembered; but for his iniquity that he hath committed, he shall die for it. . . . When the righteous turneth from his righteousness, and committeth iniquity, he shall even die thereby."

It is a weak rejoinder to say that this applies only to the destruction of the city of Jerusalem; or that it is "self-righteousness" which is mentioned here. Would it not be a deed of merit to turn from self-righteousness? Why then should people be warned of death if they turn from their self-righteousness? Above and beyond all dispensational limitations is God's eternal truth, "The soul that sinneth, it shall die" (Ezek. 18:4, 20; see also vv. 24, 30).

It is impossible to miss the relevance of Christ's words

in Matt. 18:21-35 in this connection. Here we have the parable of the two debtors, one forgiven a sum of tremendous size, but refusing to forgive a fellow servant who owed an almost insignificant amount. "His lord was wroth," we read, "and delivered him to the tormentors, till he should pay all that was due unto him" (v. 34). Then Jesus added, "*So likewise shall my heavenly Father do also unto you,* if ye from your hearts forgive not every one his brother their trespasses" (v. 35).

Matthew also records the words of Christ regarding final justification when he says, "But I say unto you, That every idle word that men shall speak, they shall give account thereof in the day of judgment. For by thy words thou shalt be justified, and by thy words thou shalt be condemned" (12:36-37). Paul echoes the same thought when he says, "For not the hearers of the law are just before God, but the doers of the law shall be justified" (Rom. 2:13).

No evangelical Christian believes that one can be justified by his good deeds. We are justified by faith, but it is a faith which brings peace with God (Rom 5:1) and the regenerating grace of Christ, which we have already seen to be incompatible with sin. Paul in Gal. 2:16 says: "Knowing that a man is not justified by the works of the law, but by the faith of Jesus Christ, even we have believed in Jesus Christ, that we might be justified by the faith of Christ, and not by the works of the law: for by the works of the law shall no flesh be justified." Then as if anticipating this opinion that justification by faith forever settles the claims of the law, and forgives all future sins, he adds: "*But if, while we seek to be justified by Christ, we ourselves also are found sinners,* is therefore Christ the minister of sin? God forbid. For if I build again the things which I destroyed, I make myself a transgressor" (vv. 17-18).

There is an amazing resemblance between this justification-before-the-act theory and the doctrine of indulgences in the Roman church which sparked the Reformation in Luther's day. Both teach that sin may be forgiven before it is committed. The false security idea goes even farther than Romanism, however, and teaches that *all* future sins are forgiven, not just the few for which indulgence might be bought.

The whole second chapter of James cries out in protest against such antinomianism (the teaching that Christians are not obliged to keep the moral law in order to remain justified). James addresses his brethren (v. 1), and says: "But if ye have respect to persons, ye commit sin, and are convinced of the law as transgressors. For whosoever shall keep the whole law, and yet offend in one point, he is guilty of all. For he that said, Do not commit adultery, said also, Do not kill. Now if thou commit no adultery, yet if thou kill, thou art become a transgressor of the law" (vv. 9-11).

With regard to Abraham, James says: "Was not Abraham our father justified by works, when he had offered Isaac his son upon the altar? Seest thou how faith wrought with his works, and by works was faith made perfect? And the scripture was fulfilled which saith, Abraham believed God, and it was imputed unto him for righteousness: and he was called the Friend of God. Ye see then how that by works a man is justified, and not by faith only" (vv. 21-24).

James here is simply saying that it is not a question of faith instead of obedience, or obedience instead of faith. It is a question of faith *and* obedience. The genuineness of faith is tested by the quality of the life of obedience. Paul himself said, "Work out your own salvation with fear and trembling. For it is God which worketh in you both to will and to do of his good pleasure" (Phil. 2:12-13).

The Apostle Paul's statement in 1 Cor. 11:29-32 is often used to support this "no judgment for the sins of believers" fancy. Here, in connection with the Lord's Supper, we read: "For he that eateth and drinketh unworthily, eateth

49

and drinketh damnation to himself, not discerning the Lord's body. For this cause many are weak and sickly among you, and many sleep. For if we would judge ourselves, we should not be judged. But when we are judged, we are chastened of the Lord, that we should not be condemned with the world."

This, it is said, supports the idea that a believer may live so vile a life on earth that he is taken to heaven—"for many sleep." God chastens His "children" for their sins, but they are not condemned with the world.

All of this overlooks one very vital little word in the thirty-second verse. We are chastened of the Lord, *that* (Greek, *in order that*) we should not be condemned with the world. The purpose of God's chastening the backslider is not to fully punish His erring "child," but to bring him to repentance and restoration, so that he be not condemned with the world. In Romans 2, Paul writes that those who judge others and are themselves guilty of sin cannot escape the judgment of God (vv. 1-3). He adds: "Or despisest thou the riches of his goodness and forbearance and longsuffering; not knowing that the goodness of God leadeth thee to repentance? But after thy hardness and impenitent heart treasurest up unto thyself wrath against the day of wrath and revelation of the righteous judgment of God; who will render to every man according to his deeds" (vv. 4-6).

There is nothing in the Bible to support the idea of one single act of justification covering all future sins. Such is pure fabrication, and a weak substitute for the regenerating and sanctifying grace of the Lord Jesus Christ in providing deliverance from sin. True security says: "Know ye not, that to whom ye yield yourselves servants to obey, his servants ye are to whom ye obey; whether of sin unto death, or of obedience unto righteousness? . . . Being then made free from sin, ye became the servants of righteousness. . . . as ye have yielded your members servants to uncleanness and to iniquity unto iniquity; even so now yield your members

50

servants to righteousness unto holiness. . . . Now being made free from sin, and become servants to God, ye have your fruit unto holiness, and the end everlasting life" (Rom. 6:16, 18-19, 22).

8

About
Dispensationalism

Dispensationalism is one of the most ingenious systems of biblical interpretation ever devised to escape the clear statements of God's inspired Word. It takes a half-truth, and by artificial and strained application transforms it into a principle of interpretation which permits almost any deduction one might wish to draw from the pages of the Book.

The half-truth with which dispensationalism starts is the obvious principle of Bible interpretation that all understanding of scripture must start with the context. "A text without a context is only a pretext." Scripture is like a railroad ticket, "Void if detached." In interpreting the Word we must consider *what* is written, *by whom* it is written, *to whom* it is addressed, and *for what purpose* the passage or book is composed.

Taking part of this principle, dispensationalists construct an artificial context of so-called "dispensations," sometimes three, more usually seven in number. These dispensations are then held to be relatively separate and distinct modes of God's dealing with men, in which the truths given in and for one dispensation are said to be inapplicable to all the others.

It may be readily admitted that there are important distinctions in the mode of God's dealings with men in the Old Testament age of ceremonial law and in the New Testament or gospel age of divine grace. For this reason, we have quoted few Old Testament passages in relation to security.

But having said this, we must immediately affirm the unity of the Bible as a whole. This is distinctly taught in the New Testament. "All scripture is given by inspiration of God, and is profitable for doctrine, for reproof, for correction, for instruction in righteousness: that the man of God may be perfect, throughly furnished unto all good works" (2 Tim. 3:16-17).

The applications of dispensationalism to security are many. A few examples may suffice, for the principle is the same in each instance. For example, the passages quoted earlier from Ezekiel (18:20-30; 33:12-13) are said to apply only to Israel under the dispensation of the law, and to have no meaning whatsoever for Christians under grace. Included in this same "explanation" is Ps. 51:11, "Cast me not away from thy presence; and take not thy holy spirit from me."

It would perhaps be convenient if all uncomfortable statements from the Bible could be thus bracketed and made to apply only to some other people or some other age. Certainly, all passages of scripture were written *to* a specific people under specific circumstances. But they were written *for* all men in all ages.

The Apostle Paul states in 1 Corinthians 10 that Old Testament history was given to us for our guidance: "Now these things were our examples, to the intent that we should not lust after evil things, as they also lusted" (v. 6); "Now all these things happened unto them for ensamples: and they are written for our admonition, upon whom the ends of the world are come" (v. 11). That Paul has those sections of the Old Testament in mind which bear upon false confidence and mistaken security is quite clear when he adds in verse 12, *"Wherefore let him that thinketh he standeth take heed lest he fall."*

In the New Testament, great portions of the scripture are laid aside as irrelevent to the "Church age" by dispensationalists. For instance, Matt. 18:23-35, previously quoted, where Jesus speaks of the king and his unforgiving servant, it is claimed, refers to a "Kingdom age" which is yet to come. Likewise, Matt. 24:13, "But he that shall endure unto the end, the same shall be saved," is said to mean only enduring through the tribulation period. These strained interpretations are made in spite of the fact that Jesus said of the unforgiving debtor, "So likewise shall my heavenly Father do also *unto you*" (v. 35); and added after His promise of final salvation to the persevering believer the words, "And this gospel of the kingdom shall be preached in all the world for a witness unto all nations; and then shall the end come" (v. 14).

God's attitude toward sin has never changed. Through every "dispensation," whether it be of conscience, of law, of the Church, of the Kingdom, or what not—indeed even from before the creation of the earth—God has declared His eternal hatred of sin. A holy Father-God turned away from His only begotten Son (Mark 15:34) when Jesus became a Sin Offering for us and bore our sins on the Cross, even though He personally was in no sense guilty of our transgressions. By what right, then, may anyone expect that this same holy God will tolerate the sinfulness of backsliding believers and cast His grace as a cloak over their unrighteousness?

Jude declares God's eternal hatred of evil, and the fact that a prior state of salvation is of no avail to those who turn aside from the way of righteousness, when he says: "For

54

there are certain men crept in unawares, who were of old ordained to this condemnation, ungodly men turning the grace of our God into lasciviousness, and denying the only Lord God, and our Lord Jesus Christ. I will therefore put you in remembrance, though ye once knew this, how that the Lord, having saved the people out of the land of Egypt, afterward destroyed them that believed not. And the angels which kept not their first estate, but left their own habitation, he hath reserved in everlasting chains under darkness unto the judgment of the great day" (vv. 4-6).

To set aside large portions of the eternal truth of God as irrelevant and not applicable to Christians today is dangerously close to what is described in Rev. 22:19, "And if any man take away from the words of the book of this prophecy, God shall take away his part out of the book of life, and out of the holy city, and from the things which are written in this book."

9

True Security

God has provided perfect security for every trusting child of His. It is a security that is real and absolute, and which perfectly vindicates the promises of His holy Word. It is "not by works of righteousness which we have done, but according to his mercy he saved us, by the washing of regeneration, *and* renewing of the Holy Ghost" (Titus 3:5). It is a security which saves and keeps the trusting soul from known and deliberate sin.

The fact that there is no security for those who, after a Christian profession, continue in or go back to sin does not lessen the safety of the truly regenerate soul. In many cases, such were never saved. "They went out from us, but they were not of us; for if they had been of us, they would no doubt have continued with us: but they went out, that they might be made manifest that they were not all of us" (1 John 2:19). Others, however, are "salt" which has lost its savor, and is "thenceforth good for nothing, but to be cast out, and to be trodden under foot of men" (Matt. 5:13). For "no man, having put his hand to the plough, and looking back, is fit for the kingdom of God" (Luke 9:62).

The search for security is a legitimate desire of every human heart. But it cannot be found in a life marred by sin and spiritual defeat. "The eyes of the Lord are over the righteous, and his ears are open unto their prayers: but the face of the Lord is against them that do evil" (1 Pet. 3:12). "If I regard iniquity in my heart, the Lord will not hear me" (Ps. 66:18). "He that turneth his ear from the hearing of the law, even his prayer shall be abomination" (Prov. 28:9). "The Lord is with you while ye be with him; and if ye seek him, he will be found of you; but if ye forsake him, he will forsake you" (2 Chron. 15:2).

To say, as some have, that "man's acts, apart from accepting the Savior, are not related to salvation and thus no act of man or demerit of man can cause him to be taken out of the condition of being saved,"[1] does not contribute to security, but only leads to fatal presumption and dependence upon a false hope. For "the fearful, and unbelieving, and the abominable, and murderers, and whoremongers, and sorcerers, and idolaters, and all liars, shall have their part in the lake which burneth with fire and brimstone: which is the second death" (Rev. 21:8), and it will not do to add "unless they were once converted." The righteous who turn back to sin will not only die once physically, but also die the second death; for "when a righteous man turneth away from his righteousness, and committeth iniquity, and dieth in them; for his iniquity that he hath done shall he die" (Ezek. 18:26).

True security depends, for one thing, upon a complete repudiation of self-confidence and softness toward sin. With Paul we may say, "We then, as workers together with him, beseech you also that ye receive not the grace of God in vain" (2 Cor. 6:1). "Stand fast therefore in the liberty wherewith Christ hath made us free, and be not entangled again with the yoke of bondage. . . . Christ is become of no effect unto you, whosoever of you are justified by the law; ye are fallen

57

from grace" (Gal. 5:1, 4). "Nevertheless I have somewhat against thee, because thou hast left thy first love. Remember therefore from whence thou art fallen, and repent, and do the first works; or else I will come unto thee quickly, and will remove thy candlestick out of his place, except thou repent" (Rev. 2:4-5).

It is possible to put this matter of security on the basis of "safety first." The doctrine of unconditional eternal security is either true or false. If it is true, it holds for every person who has ever savingly believed on the Lord Jesus Christ, whether he accepts this view or not. If, on the other hand, it is false, then backsliders who live out their lives in sin are forever and hopelessly lost.

Conversely, the doctrine that the security of the believer is conditioned on his continued faith and obedience is either true or false. If it is true, then those who live by it will be saved by the grace of the Lord Jesus Christ. However, if it is false, they will still be saved. Thus, whether right or wrong, he who believes in and lives by the doctrine of conditional Christian security is safe.

There are also serious objections to holding a theory by which one cannot live. Preachers of eternal security do not advocate a life of sin, although they make it possible within the framework of a hope of eternal salvation. They point out that even premature death may be the Father's discipline for a sinning "saint." Yet is not this a rather oblique way of saying that the more you sin the quicker you will get to heaven? To say, as others do, that those who interpret the theory in this fashion thereby give evidence that they are strangers to the grace of God would seem only to penalize the consistent soul who is not afraid to follow through on the implications of his beliefs!

On the other hand, true security safeguards against carelessness. It makes no compromise with sin. It leads to a life of holiness, made possible by the dynamic of divine grace. It is a theory by which the humblest child of God may walk, and wherein he is absolutely secure, whether his theory is true or false. This, to say the least, is something to ponder carefully.

By this time, the path of true security should have become plain. It involves two simple but fundamental acts of divine grace. The first is the regenerating work of the divine Spirit, by which the "power of canceled sin" is broken, by virtue of which "sin shall not have dominion over you: for ye are not under the law, but under grace" (Rom. 6:14).

The second is to "follow peace with all men, and holiness, without which no man shall see the Lord: looking diligently lest any man fail of [marg., 'fall back from'] the grace of God; lest any root of bitterness springing up trouble you, and thereby many be defiled; lest there be any fornicator, or profane person, as Esau, who for one morsel of meat sold his birthright" (Heb. 12:14-16).

Throughout the New Testament, the preserving power of the Holy Spirit is closely related to His work of sanctification. In His great high-priestly prayer in John 17, Jesus prays, "not that thou shouldest take them out of the world, but that thou shouldest keep them from the evil. They are not of the world, even as I am not of the world. Sanctify them through thy truth: thy word is truth. . . . Neither pray I for these alone, but for them also which shall believe on me through their word" (vv. 15-17, 20).

Likewise Paul writes in 1 Thess. 5:23-24: "And the very God of peace sanctify you wholly; and I pray God your whole spirit and soul and body be preserved blameless unto the coming of our Lord Jesus Christ. Faithful is he that calleth you, who also will do it."

It is through "sanctification of the Spirit" (1 Pet. 1:2) that believers are cleansed of inner sin, and thereby assured the possibility of complete victory over outer sin, and a witness which is powerful because consistent. "Even as Christ also loved the church, and gave himself for it; that he might sanctify and cleanse it with the washing of water by the word, that he might present it to himself a glorious church, not having spot, or wrinkle, or any such thing; but that it should be holy and without blemish" (Eph. 5:25-27). "Knowing this, that our old man is crucified with him, that the body of sin might be destroyed, that henceforth we should not serve sin" (Rom. 6:6). "But ye shall receive power, after that the Holy Ghost is come upon you: and ye shall be witnesses unto me both in Jerusalem, and in all Judaea, and in Samaria, and unto the uttermost part of the earth" (Acts 1:8).

It is tragic that false teaching has paralyzed the faith of so many of God's children. They have been taught to live in the seventh chapter of Romans, groaning: "I am carnal, sold under sin. For that which I do I allow not: for what I would, that do I not; but what I hate, that do I. . . . For the good that I would I do not: but the evil which I would not, that I do. . . . I find then a law, that, when I would do good, evil is present with me. For I delight in the law of God after the inward man: but I see another law in my members, warring against the law of my mind, and bringing me into captivity to the law of sin which is in my members. O wretched man that I am! who shall deliver me from the body of this death?" (vv. 14-15, 19, 21-24).

It is little wonder that those who hold such a limited view of the power of Christ's gospel should seek a substitute for the victorious life in the doctrine of unconditional eternal security. How much better to recognize that Paul's gospel does not end at Rom. 7:25, but reaches its climax in Rom. 8:2, where he says, "For the law of the *Spirit of life* in Christ Jesus *hath made me free* from the law of sin and death."

Likewise, the true gospel of Christ refuses to stop with Gal. 5:17, "For the flesh lusteth against the Spirit, and the Spirit against the flesh: and these are contrary the one to the other: so that ye cannot do the things that ye would." It goes on to Gal. 5:22-24, "But the fruit of the Spirit is love, joy, peace, longsuffering, gentleness, goodness, faith, meekness, temperance: against such there is no law. *And they that are Christ's have crucified the flesh* with the affections and lusts."

God's security program, therefore, works from within through the dynamic of the sanctifying Spirit. It is INTERNAL SECURITY. "Who shall ascend into the hill of the Lord? or who shall stand in his holy place? He that hath clean hands, and a pure heart; who hath not lifted up his soul unto vanity, nor sworn deceitfully" (Ps. 24:3-4). "Cleanse your hands, ye sinners; and purify your hearts, ye double minded" (Jas. 4:8). "Having therefore these promises, dearly beloved, let us cleanse ourselves from all filthiness of the flesh and spirit, perfecting holiness in the fear of God" (2 Cor. 7:1). "And God, which knoweth the hearts, bare them witness, giving them the Holy Ghost, even as he did unto us; and put no difference between us and them, purifying their hearts by faith" (Acts 15:8-9).

A pure heart, issuing in a clean life and consecrated service, is the completely adequate security provided for the children of God. One of the great summations of the gospel to be found in the New Testament is given in 2 Pet. 1:2-11. Here is maximum security, outlined by God's inspired penman:

"Grace and peace be multiplied unto you through the knowledge of God, and of Jesus our Lord, according as his divine power hath given unto us all things that pertain unto life and godliness, through the knowledge of him that hath called us to glory and virtue: whereby are given unto us exceeding great and precious promises: that by these ye might be partakers of the divine nature, having escaped the corruption that is in the world through lust.

"*And beside all this,* giving all diligence, add to your

faith virtue; and to virtue knowledge; and to knowledge temperance; and to temperance patience; and to patience godliness; and to godliness brotherly kindness; and to brotherly kindness charity.

"*For if these things be in you and abound*, they make you that ye shall neither barren nor unfruitful in the knowledge of our Lord Jesus Christ. But he that lacketh these things is blind, and cannot see afar off, and hath forgotten that he was purged from his old sins.

"Wherefore the rather, brethren, give diligence to make your calling and election *sure: for if ye do these things, ye shall never fall:* for so an entrance shall be ministered unto you abundantly into the everlasting kingdom of our Lord and Saviour Jesus Christ."

Reference Notes

CHAPTER 3

1. John R. Rice, *Can a Saved Person Ever Be Lost?* (Murphreesboro, Tenn.: Sword of the Lord Publishers, n.d.), p. 16.

2. H. A. Ironside, *The Eternal Security of the Believer* (New York: Loizeaux Bros., 1934), p. 6.

CHAPTER 4

1. Rice, *Can a Saved Person Ever Be Lost?* p. 17.

CHAPTER 6

1. August Van Ryn, *The Epistles of John* (New York: Loiseaux Bros., 1948), *loc. cit.*

CHAPTER 7

1. Ironside, *Security of the Believer*, p. 10.

2. *Ibid.*, p. 11.

CHAPTER 9

1. J. F. Strombeck, *Shall Never Perish* (Chicago: Moody Press, 1966), p. 28.

Index to Scripture References